Psilocybin Mushrooms

A Comprehensive Guide to Growing and Using Psychedelic Mushrooms

Table of Contents

Introduction 1

Chapter One: History of Psilocybin Mushrooms 4

Chapter Two: Understanding Psilocybin Mushrooms 10

Chapter Three: The Science of Psilocybin Mushrooms 17

Chapter Four: Grow Kits 27

Chapter Five: How to Grow Psilocybin Mushrooms 34

Chapter Six: Health Benefits of Psilocybin Mushrooms 49

Final Words 54

Introduction

Mushrooms are mushrooms, not plants that exist in another class side by side. They grow from spores, usually in decaying materials from plants, in the ground, or on things like logs. Some mushrooms contain minute life and nutrients used to add an earthy flavor and meaty texture to everything from pizza to risotto. "Psilocybin mushrooms" is the generic name given to mushrooms that contain psilocybin (a natural psychedelic compound). Psilocybin is a hallucinogenic substance. "Psilocybin" mushrooms are often defined by the fact that they contain psilocybin, a compound with hallucinogenic effects that alters perception.

Psilocybin mushrooms have been used under therapeutic conditions to treat a wide range of ailments, including obsessive-compulsive disorder, cluster headache, anxiety, addiction, and depression. Psilocybin mushrooms have a long history of use in Mesoamerica in spiritual and religious rituals. They are also currently one of the most popular recreational psychedelics in Europe and the United States. These mushrooms are famous for the psychedelic effects they have on those who eat them, and also for the antediluvian practice dating back to prehistoric "mushroom cults" and the shamans who could have inspired Santa Claus. Archaeological findings from the Sahara suggest that people have been using hallucinogenic mushrooms for over 7000 years. Fungi are represented in the prehistoric art of different geographic regions. They are sometimes religiously symbolic, especially in the context of various rights and ceremonies. The Psilocybin mushroom grows in much of South America, Mexico, Malaysia, Indonesia, and India, although you can also find them in eastern Australia and the southern United States.

It is thought that they have been available for thousands of years in religious rites and that the Aztecs certainly knew about them.

Additionally, Psilocybin mushrooms are widely viewed as a possible miraculous psychiatric drug. Studies have shown promising effects in treating depression. For example, a 2017 survey shows that psilocybin "can successfully restore the activity of important brain circuits that are known to play a role in depression." They appear to stimulate emotional reactivity in the brain. A recent study suggests that Psilocybin mushrooms can relieve depression without the same side effects associated with antidepressants and Selective Serotonin Reuptake Inhibitors (SSRIs). In recent years, regulatory agencies such as the FDA and DEA have loosened the rules on the use of psilocybin in controlled scientific studies more than any other psychedelic. A new survey of psilocybin uses it as a tool of Thera-potica and as part of personal/spiritual development methods. Psychedelic mushrooms are divided into two categories, and each type is categorized by a different mix of ingredients that make it a "Psilocybin mushroom." There are over 180 species of Psilocybin mushrooms all over the world. In fact, the only continent where they don't grow is Antarctica. Many species also contain psilocin, another similar compound to psilocybin.

These various mushrooms come from a dozen genera. Nonetheless, they are often grouped as "psilocybin mushrooms." Many of these species fit the family Psilocybe, including the species known as psilocybin cubensis ("golden cap") and psilocybin semilanceata ("cover of freedom"). Psilocybin fungi can be very different according to recent studies because psilocybin genes are not inherited from a mutual ancestor but are directly transferred between unrelated species in a spectacle named "horizontal gene transmission." Psilocybin may have developed as a defense mechanism for the mushroom, which discourages parasites "that feed on insects" to change their mind.

Magic mushrooms, wild or cultivated, are mushrooms containing 'psilocybin,' the main hallucinogenic psychoactive component. They are considered a Class I drug, which means they have a high potential for misuse and have not been widely accepted for medical use in the

United States. In addition to being labeled as magic mushrooms, they are also known as mushrooms, molds, blue meanders, golden tops, caps for freedom, blocks, and freedom. Magic mushrooms are often dried and consumed by mixing them in food or drink, although some people eat freshly picked magic mushrooms.

Psilocybin mushrooms are known to cause hallucinations, a sense of belonging to nature, a feeling of sleep or relaxation, and introspection, but they can also produce effects such as nervousness, terror, and paranoia. These types of mushrooms commonly look like normal mushrooms with long, thin stems. They can be whitish-gray and dark brown, light brown, or white in color.

These mushrooms are often mixed with milk or drunk like tea and can also be consumed with marijuana or tobacco. Liquid psilocybin, the natural mystical material found in Liberty capsules, is also available. In this rare case, the dark brown liquid is supplied in a small ampoule. Magic mushrooms are hallucinogenic drugs, which means they can make you see, hear and perceive hallucinations that seem real but are not. However, magic mushroom experiences are highly variable and believed to be influenced by environmental factors. These substances have a long history of being associated with spiritual experiences and self-discovery. Many people argue that natural substances like psilocybin mushrooms, marijuana, and mescaline are sacred medicines that allow people to reach higher spiritual states. Others take these mushrooms to simply experience euphoria, empathy, and a distorted sense of time.

Chapter One: History of Psilocybin Mushrooms

Everything has a beginning - scientists have even been able to compile evidence that the Universe has a beginning, and it's still expanding at this present moment. Psilocybin Mushrooms became widely known after R. W. Gordon's "rediscovery" of the shamanic use of Psilocybin-containing mushrooms back in the 1950s in Mexico. At this time, the science behind growing mushrooms, either indoors or outdoors, was still in its infancy. The only Mushroom species prevailing in the West around that time wasn't the Psilocybe but the Agaricus Bisporus. They called it the common white button mushroom. The methods used for growing the common white button mushrooms were closely related to the ones used in France during the 17th century. Things were very much wild during those times: Growers would get their mushrooms from the wild, then bring them back home. They would grow them in rows of horse manure in mycelium-rich soil, usually in a naturally climate-controlled cave. Instruments of science were in their infancy during these times. Hence, even though the method worked, issues with unpasteurized substrate often contaminated the process.

This method was used all through the 20th century until several incremental improvements in Biology started setting in. The advancements in science began to strategically promote the Bisporus mushroom species and gave room for the Almighty Psilocybe Cubensis in the 1960s.

Some years after Falconer published his book, several scientists later discovered something inspiring and exciting. The associated afflictions linked to mushroom growing were eradicated by using Horse manure that was subjected to heat sterilization before being inoculated with Agaricus mycelium. Have you ever heard the word "spawn" among mushroom growers before? After discovering what happened right after Falconer's book was published, the essence of the first pure mushroom spawns was formed. You might be aware that Pennsylvania State College is by far the leading center of mushroom growing research and home to James W. Sinden, a mycologist who works at the Pennsylvania state college. Sinden discovered that sterilized wheat could contribute more growth to mushrooms. He stated that sterilized wheat grain is more effective and robust.

The Biology of Psilocybin Mushrooms

The physical characteristics of psilocybin mushrooms are the straight stem, open flat cap, width, and the dark brown color. Inexperienced people cannot correctly recognize Psilocybin mushrooms; they might mix them up with other types of mushrooms. Many mushrooms are poisonous and can cause death. Therefore, inexperienced people should not search for psilocybin mushrooms without expert help.

These mushrooms are mainly identified by their white gills. These gills have linings in which spores are present. These spores are responsible for the spread of these mushrooms through different dispersal procedures. However, not all gilled mushrooms are Psilocybin mushrooms. Psilocybin mushrooms have brown or black spores inside the gills, and sometimes these mushrooms have bluish bruises.

They have the same internal structure as other fungi. There is a cap attached to a stem, containing gills inside. These gills have spores inside. The stem is attached to the volva, and the volva stands on hyphae, the hair-like structures protruding out, which attaches this mushroom to the ground, and is called mycelium. Almost all fungi have this structure, with few exceptions.

The Life Cycle of Psilocybin Mushrooms

The hyphae of mycelia of magic mushrooms pass through plasmogamy. Plasmogamy is a process in which the cytoplasm from two different parent cells fuses but leaves the nuclei infused. This means cytoplasm combines, but nuclei remain haploid. Psilocybin mushrooms have haploid gametes, i.e., (n) instead of (2n). They form a diploid mycelium from a haploid parent. When the environment is suitable, this mycelium grows into mushrooms. When karyogamy occurs in the cells, it results in the formation of gills. Karyogamy is a process in which the two unfused haploid nuclei fuse to form diploid nuclei. To understand the life cycle of Psilocybin mushrooms, keep these points in mind:

- Spores release and disperse through the wind.
- Spores find a suitable environment and germinate.
- Mating occurs.
- Plasmogamy occurs.
- Dikaryotic mycelium.
- Gills form containing basidia.
- Haploid nuclei.
- Karyogamy occurs.
- Diploid nuclei form.
- Meiosis occurs (formation of basidiospores).
- Release of spores.
- The cycle continues.

With slight differences, all mushrooms go through this life cycle. The internal structure and chemistry of all mushrooms are the same, with some small differences. For example, Psilocybin mushrooms contain Psilocybe, and it is present in these mushrooms due to horizontal gene transfer.

Identification of Psilocybin Mushrooms

Many people mix up these mushrooms with other mushrooms. To identify Psilocybin mushrooms, high expertise and experience are required. Incorrect identifications can lead to illness and even death.

Hofmann and his team were the first who identified the Psilocybin mushrooms successfully using laboratory methods. These identifications were made in 1958. Before that, people used to identify these mushrooms only through their outer look and assumptions. But Hofmann and his team members changed the game. They used Psilocybe Mexicana to grow its cultures in the laboratory and then grow its fruiting bodies, sclerotia, and mycelium using these cultures. They also observed that the same psychoactive activity was present in both dried and fresh samples of Psilocybe Mexicana. That was when the compounds behind the psychoactive activity and hallucinogenic properties of these mushrooms were discovered. Improper identification of mushrooms may lead to death, so one must understand the shape and structure of psilocybe mushrooms to avoid misidentifications. As these mushrooms have hallucinogenic properties, they can alter the human mind, thus producing intense psychological effects. These effects can be for a short period or more prolonged, depending upon the quantity of mushroom taken and the power of that specific mushroom.

To identify magic mushrooms, one must consider these points:

- Brown in color mushrooms (bodies are brown fruiting)
- White gills on the underside
- Many psilocybe mushrooms have a ring around their necks
- Bacterium color (typically purple-colored spores for psilocybe mushrooms)

This is not the ultimate guide for mushroom identification, so if you find such mushrooms and need to identify if they are magic mushrooms or not, ideally you would check them in a laboratory to confirm. You can also use spore printing as an easy method to identify those mushrooms. Use a piece of paper, put spores on them, and check the color they leave on tissue paper. This method can help to identify the psilocybin mushrooms. Thus, two essential methods of mushroom identification are:

- Spore printing
- Bluing reaction

Spore Printing

Spore color is the most crucial factor in mushroom identification. If you are a mushroom collector or are searching for psilocybe mushrooms for some purpose, consider their spores. Take the mushrooms and put them in polythene bags, but remember, don't tighten the bags because they have to breathe. If mushrooms become dry, the spores will change their color, which will not help in identification. So, use fresh and live mushrooms.

Open the polythene bag, take a mushroom, and cut it. There is a proper way to cut these mushrooms. Choose flattened mushrooms to cut and separate their caps from the stem using a knife. Put the gills of the mushrooms (underside of the cap) on the paper or tissue paper and cover it with some glass to increase the level of hydration and decrease the chance of dehydration. Keeping the air currents away will give a good spore print. If the gills are humid or wet, they will provide a good spore print. If they leave purple or dark purple color on tissue paper, they are likely psilocybin mushrooms. This process is called spore printing because it leaves its print on tissue paper for identification purposes. According to the symmetry of the gills, the spores will print on the paper, showing the mass and color of the spores. After identification, you can label the print, and also, you can use these spore prints for mushroom cultivation in the future.

Bluing Reaction

The second critical strategy to identify psilocybe mushrooms is their bluing reaction. Many psilocybe mushrooms have common properties that become the source of their identification. Most of the psilocybe mushrooms become bluish or bluish-green when they are bruised. Mushrooms don't get bruises only when they are crushed. Mushrooms can get bluish bruises when they are handled or picked. This bluing reaction shows that there is something different in these mushrooms. Scientists and researchers are in search of finding the reasons behind this bluing reaction. One reason behind this bluing is the degradation of the psilocybe compound and psilocin. Some other unknown compounds also participate in this reaction. This is the most important identifying factor of Psilocybin mushrooms as most other mushrooms do not have this property. But, on the other hand, some psilocybe species don't show this blue color or bluish bruises. After some time, researchers have found that there are some poisonous mushrooms with bluish bruises, but they have no psilocybe. For example, the Hygrophorus conicus is a poisonous mushroom species that shows a bluish reaction when picking it up. So, you have to be careful when it comes to identification.

Chapter Two: Understanding Psilocybin Mushrooms

Psilocybin mushrooms are specific types of mushrooms that naturally contain psychedelic compounds; therefore. Psilocybin is the main component found in various psychoactive mushrooms, making it perhaps the most well-known natural psychedelic drug. Although psilocybin is considered active at doses of about 3-4 mg, a typical dosage used in clinical research settings varies from 14-30 mg. The brain symptoms it causes are due to its active metabolite, psilocin.

Most commonly found in natural or cultivated mushrooms, psilocybin is marketed either fresh or dried. Psilocybe cubensis, the most prominent species of psilocybin mushrooms, is usually taken orally either by consuming dried caps and stems or steeped in hot water and drank as a tea, with a typical dose of about 1-2.5 grams. Psilocybin mushrooms are a type of mushrooms known on ingestion to produce strong psychedelic effects. Mushrooms are a fungus, which means they emerge from spores that create mycelium networks into the soil or rotting plant matter, like old logs. When the setting is right, a fungus, like a flora, will flower. These are the mushrooms we pick.

Psychoactive mushroom varieties most commonly fall under the genus Psilocybin. This genus includes more than 200 mushroom varieties, all of which contain psilocybin, the main active compound responsible for producing psychoactive effects. Other mushroom varieties also cause psychedelic effects, for example, the fly amanita. Psilocybin mushrooms, however, are the most popular by far. On average, one single mushroom will contain psilocybin between 0.2 and 0.4 percent.

The Most Common Psilocybin Mushrooms

In many countries all over the world, psilocybin-containing mushrooms are available. Archeological investigations sometimes find examples of magic mushrooms or connections to them. Commentators such as the late Terence McKenna indicated that early hominids who consumed magic mushrooms were inspired to create a sophisticated language and religion, contributing to more complex cultures. There is no doubt that psilocybin is a great drug, but please be careful if you collect wild mushrooms. Correct identification is critical in general when working with the fungi. A few poisonous varieties mimic a variety of magic mushrooms. Adverse reactions will range from mild diarrhea to anaphylaxis and sometimes even death. Please be 100% certain before ingesting food that has not been produced from known spores.

At maximum, heading into the forest is reckless and, at worst, suicidal, picking up those mystery shrooms and swallowing them. The mushroom you want will have specific conditions it thrives under. The critical factors are temperature, humidity, medium development, and the time of year. It's also essential to know your target's life cycle. Based on parent mycelium, the fruiting body usually only exists for a few months or appears every few years. There are thousands of mushroom species in the world, but because of their hallucinogenic properties, Psilocybin Mushrooms have become more common.

Psilocybe Mushrooms

Psilocybe is a type of mushroom best known for its psychoactive compounds: psilocybin, and biocytin.

Typically, the fruit bodies of the mushrooms that belong to this group are small and are distinguished by their small to medium caps, brown to yellow coloration, and a spore-print varying from lilac brown to dark purple-gray. Likewise, this sort of magic mushroom appears to bruise when treated.

All organisms belonging to this group grow on organic matter, which is rotting. Psychedelic effects occur 20-60 minutes after Psilocybe cubensis has been swallowed, and these results can last from 4-10 hours. Such results include optical distortion, vivid color enhancement, and realistic forms of animation. Varieties of mushrooms that belong to the Psilocybe group include the following:

Psilocybin Cubensis. Possibly the most common of all Psilocybes, this species is also known as shrooms or cubes, with diversity is rising throughout the globe. In the United States, Gulf Coast, Brazil, Central America, South America, West Indies, Vietnam, Indonesia, Asia, and Australia, it grows on cow dung. Thanks to their conic to convex caps, which can expand from 2 and 8 cm in diameter anywhere, they can be easily identified. Their reddish-cinnamon color transforms with age to a golden brown, contributing to their street name, gold hats. This includes psilocybin, biocytin, and psilocin. The concentrations of each material in this species differ, owing to factors such as age.

Psilocybe Cyanescens. This form is also known as wavy caps because of their tops, which, when maturing, are wavy. Because of its light buff and yellowish color, the caps are quite distinctive within its class. These also have very characteristic blackish-brown spores. In the US, P. Cyanescens spreads south of the San Francisco Bay area in the Pacific Northwest. It also develops throughout Western and Central Africa, Canada, Western Asia, Western Europe, Central Europe, and New Zealand. It extends along the perimeters of urban areas and grows in mulched beds on woodchips. Because of the fruiting needs of this species, it isn't easy to grow them indoors.

Psilocybe Semilanceata. This fungus grows in grasslands and especially in wetlands. In comparison to P. Cubensis, it does not develop on dung. It feeds on diminishing grassroots and is distributed in 17 northern hemisphere countries, especially in North America, Canada, Russia, Switzerland, Poland, and the Netherlands.

They are often known as the caps of liberty or semilanceata. Their caps range from distinctly conical to bell-shaped, with a pronounced tip that looks like a breast.

Psilocybe Azurescens. This is the most active psilocybin-containing mushrooms with amounts of 1.78 percent psilocybin. People new to magic mushrooms should, for the first time, avoid eating more than an 8th of a P. Azurescens. The variety is incredibly robust and twice as effective as the P. Cubensis. The cap has a diameter of 30-100 mm and flattens with age. They are found along a small area of the West Coast of the United States, among coastal dune grasses. A handful of endangered species are also in Germany.

Conocybe Mushrooms

Some forms of monocyte mushrooms have long, thin, delicate stems, which thrive on dead vegetation, dead grass, sand dunes, decayed trees, and dung in rich grasslands. Thanks to their conical or bell-shaped caps, Conocybe members are called coneheads. The genus monocyte contains at least 243 varieties of mushrooms, four of which contain psilocin and psilocybin, the hallucinogenic compounds:

Conocybe kehneriana. Not much of this fungus is recognized, but it occurs in Norway and Argentina. Its physical appearance is similar to that of those belonging to genus Conocybe.

Conocybe siligineoids. This fungus is also known as cone caps and is thin, low, and only around 3 inches in height. The hat is reddish-orange with a bell-shaped body. It has a rusty color as spores develop. In other parts of the world, it is hardly ever seen. They are only found in Mexico, where they were originally reported to be a medicinal mushroom used in healing and numerous other ceremonies. They are either eaten fresh or drunk in the form of tea by the locals.

Conocybe cyanopus/Pholiotina cyanopus. Currently, this fungus is allocated to the genus Pholiotina but was changed to genus Conocybe in 1935. It is a tiny mushroom with a conic to a narrowly convex cap that grows on decaying matter and is cinnamon-brown colored and smooth. It is relatively small, with striped margins typically less than 25 mm wide. The base is flat and delicate at the bottom with whitish areas, and the rest is brownish.

Spores are gray with cinnamon as well. Because of its strong resemblance to toxic plants, most mycologists warn against gathering and consuming this plant. Another feature of this species is its Sclerotia capacitance, a sleeping shape in the fruiting body that grows underground. Sclerotia are commonly called truffles. In the temperate regions of North America, Australia, Belgium, Denmark, Finland, France, Germany, Hungary, Latvia, the Netherlands, Norway, Poland, Russia, Sweden, Canada, Ukraine, and the United States, this plant occurs throughout lawns, parks and grassy areas.

Conocybe smithii/Pholiotina smithii. This mushroom has been reclassified into the genus Pholiotina. P. smithii is found in North America in moors, ditches, and sumptuous fields of sphagnum moose. It is located around the banks of the river and on lawns, too. It is known to occur in northern Michigan, Alberta, California, Wisconsin, Idaho, and historic human-made earthen mounds. It bears fruit in the early summer.

The caps of the smithii measure 0.3-1 cm across with a conic to convex form that grows almost smooth with age. Its cinnamon-brown color matches the color of its spores.

Thanks to their resemblance to poisonous mushrooms, authorities warn firmly against their use in psychedelic studies, given their slight hallucinogenic effects.

Copelandia/Panaeolus Mushrooms

Copelandia is a genus consisting of 12 varieties of mushrooms, all known to contain psilocin and psilocybin hallucinogens. American and European mycologists also decided to list within Panaeolus all members of the genus Copelandia.

Mushrooms of the genus Panaeolus are white to gray or brown, with large, thin, delicate stalks. They are distributed throughout both hemisphere's tropics and neotropics, emerging in grasslands, dry vegetation, dying grass, sand dunes, decayed trees, and dung. They continue to bruise and turn blue owing to their psilocin material.

Representative organisms within the genus Panaeolus are:

Panaeolus cambodginiensis. This is a potent hallucinogenic mushroom with both psilocybin and psilocin in it. The convex-shaped hat is less than 23 mm long. The shape of the cap is flat, and it has gills that are gray to black in color. This is in line with its black spores, too. It grows on water buffalo dung and was first seen in Cambodia but has proven to be a common occurrence across the subtropics of Asia and Hawaii.

Panaeolus cyanescens. This is another psilocybin mushroom of the group mentioned above. The tip, when small, is 1.5-4 cm across with an incurved edge. The color is yellow or brownish, but when impaired, it turns green or blue. The spores are plain black. It is also seen in habitats populated by dung that frequent pastures in Europe, India, areas of Asia, North America, and South America.

Panaeolus bisporus. This specimen visually looks no different from the P. Cambodginiensis. It can be identified only under a microscope. The thin brown fungus grows in dung and has black spores. It is located in Hawaii, southern California, North Africa, Switzerland, and Spain.

Panaeolus tropicalis. This is one of the most active psilocybin mushrooms under the family Copelandia/Panaeolus. The cap is 1.5-2.5 cm wide, clay-colored, and is hemispheric to convex. The stem is about 5-12 cm long, becoming blackish towards the middle. When it is scratched, it turns blue.

Tropical, it often grows on dung and is most frequently found in Hawaii, Cambodia, and Central Africa. Growth can also be seen in China, Uganda, the Philippines, Florida, and Japan.

Chapter Three: The Science of Psilocybin Mushrooms

Before growing or ingesting psilocybin mushrooms, it is crucial to understand the science behind them. This will help you use them in a much safer manner and have the ability to grow them more efficiently. We will discuss the chemical compound that all psychedelic mushrooms contain (psilocybin), and then we will take a look at some of the recent scientific research around this topic.

The Science Behind Psilocybin

Psilocybin is the chemical compound contained in magic mushrooms that gives them their psychedelic effects. This compound is an organic compound, as it occurs naturally in nature. It is made up of carbon, hydrogen, nitrogen, and phosphorous elements, which are all elements found on the periodic table that are found in virtually every living thing on the planet.

The psilocybin in magic mushrooms is an adaptation that certain mushrooms developed over time thanks to natural selection, a process whereby a living thing will evolve to possess certain traits that lead to its survival. This adaptation formed because ants were eating certain mushrooms. Because of this, they would die off much quicker than they usually would if it were not for the ants eating them. As a result, they developed psilocybin, which causes ants to feel full shortly after they begin to eat the mushrooms. This protects the mushrooms from taking too much damage as a result of being eaten. Psilocybin, however, has a very different effect on humans when they eat these mushrooms. This effect is the feeling of getting high. When a person ingests psilocybin, it is converted in their stomach and intestines to another chemical that is called psilocin. Psilocin then changes things happening in the brain, which is how the person begins to feel the hallucinogenic effects of the mushrooms.

When psilocybin is converted to psilocin, it acts in the brain on the receptors designed to work with the chemical serotonin, which is responsible for feelings of happiness and satisfaction. Abnormal levels of serotonin in the brain are what is responsible for depression. This explains why ingesting magic mushrooms can make a person feel elated and extreme joy. Further, psilocin leads to something that scientists call a Neuronal Avalanche, which is their way of saying that it leads to a large number of changes in the brain that keep increasing, one after the other, in a sort of domino effect. This domino effect includes changes in perception and a decreased level of normal activity within the brain, which leads to feelings of being outside of oneself or feeling the release of the "ego." What psilocybin does in the brain in terms of affecting its activity is that it increases communication among different brain areas with each other. Normally, these brain areas work pretty much independently from each other, each serving its own functions. When psilocybin is present, however, these areas suddenly begin to communicate more than they normally would, and they begin to work in harmony or tandem with one another. This release of the ego can lead to the resolution of many problems, such as mental health issues like depression. We will look at the use of magic mushrooms to treat several mental health disorders later on in this book.

Psilocybin vs. Other Psychedelic Plants or Drugs

Magic Mushrooms are part of the hallucinogenic family of drugs, including LSD, Ketamine, Salvia, and PCP. A hallucinogenic drug is classified as a substance that changes a person's perception, thoughts, and mood.

Psilocybin acts similarly to other hallucinogens, as they all mimic chemicals that are already found in the brain of humans. Psilocybin falls into the category of a Classic Hallucinogen (also included in this category is LSD). This means that it acts by imitating the body's naturally occurring processes and chemicals to enhance specific feelings or moods. There is another type of hallucinogen called a Dissociative Drug, which also acts in the brain but in a different way. This type of hallucinogen affects the brain by interfering with the chemical in the brain called Glutamate. This chemical is responsible for learning and forming memories in the human brain. Dissociative hallucinogens such as Ketamine and PCP lead to an increase in glutamate release by the brain's cells. This can lead the person to feel relaxed, slow, and put into a trance, which can lead to the relief of pain. Some individuals enjoy this forced slow-down that Ketamine and other dissociative drugs lead to if they suffer from anxiety or depression.

Similarities and Differences Between Psilocybin Mushrooms and Lysergic Acid Diethylamide (LSD)

Many people wonder about the differences between the two most common hallucinogenic drugs - LSD and Magic Mushrooms. They are both considered classic hallucinogens, so what is the difference between them and the difference between the type of trip you would have on each of them?

Similarities between Lysergic Acid Diethylamide (LSD) and Magic Mushrooms

These hallucinogenic drugs share common effects, such as feelings of unity, peace, happiness, and gratitude. Both of them have been reported as providing spiritual experiences. Another similarity is that they are both derived from a type of fungus. Mushrooms are fungus themselves, while LSD comes from a fungus found on rye, which you may know from the rye bread you can find in the grocery store. Both LSD and magic mushrooms do not inherently pose a risk for a physical addiction developing, which sets them apart from many other Schedule 1 substances. This is one of the reasons why many people argue that these two substances should not be considered illegal.

Differences between Lysergic Acid Diethylamide (LSD) and Magic Mushrooms

- One of the significant differences, though, is that LSD is created by humans. In contrast, magic mushrooms have been growing since the beginning of time and are naturally occurring, meaning that they will continue to grow without any help from humans. LSD was first created in 1938, which, compared to mushrooms, is very late, as they have been being ingested by humans since at least 9000 BC.

- Another difference is that mushrooms are legal in some places in the United States and in the world, where LSD is deemed an illicit drug.

- Another major difference is how they are ingested, as mushrooms are eaten whole, and LSD is ingested as a tab on a paper that the person will then put on their tongue or in a liquid form. Mushrooms begin acting as they are being digested. For this reason, mushrooms have more of a delayed onset when compared to LSD, as something that is absorbed in the mouth will always be much faster acting than something that must pass through the digestive tract to be absorbed.

- People report that LSD has absolutely no taste, while the taste of psychedelic mushrooms is notoriously strong.

- A typical trip on LSD can last between 8 and 12 hours, whereas a trip on magic mushrooms will last about 6-8 hours.

- One difference reported in the trip on LSD versus magic mushrooms is that people who ingest magic mushrooms feel a spiritual connection to the earth and the universe. In contrast, people who consume LSD usually feel happiness and a sense of positivity within their own lives and experiences.

When people take LSD, they will rarely have hallucinations. Even though it is considered a hallucinogen, it is known more for its effects on the brain than the actual prevalence of hallucinations. When people ingest magic mushrooms, however, it is much more common to have hallucinations. People take LSD to see things more clearly than they did when they were not on the drug. People on Magic Mushrooms may imagine objects completely and may see objects move that are not moving in reality.

The Science Behind Psilocybin Mushrooms and Therapeutic Properties

Researchers in the field of mental health and depression have theorized that for some people, depression can be caused by having lower than normal levels of substances such as neurotransmitters in the human brain, and this can cause depression. Restoring some of these brain chemicals and finding a healthy balance can alleviate some people's depression symptoms. This is where medication such as antidepressants or other therapeutic methods such as psychedelic mushrooms come in.

This theory seems to be the simplest to tackle. I mean, it's just a matter of biology, math, and a doctor's prescription that can get someone back on track, right? Wrong. Although it does seem simple, depression is a highly complex condition to treat. Just because a person successfully treated their depression using medication doesn't mean that the next person can find success with the same method. Even a treatment method for someone that has worked successfully may slowly begin to lower its effectiveness over time or even stop working completely. This happens for numerous reasons that scientists are still trying to comprehend. Researchers are still heavily invested in this area of science to continue to understand the mechanisms of depression more deeply, including chemicals in our brains, with the hope of finding more explanations and evidence for these complexities to continue developing more treatment methods for people.

For simplicity's sake, the chemical 'messengers' in our brain are called neurotransmitters. The nerve cells within our brain use these "messengers," a.k.a. Neurotransmitters, to communicate with one another. We believe that the messages that they send play a considerable role in a person's mood regulation. The three neurotransmitters that are responsible for depression are:

- Dopamine
- Serotonin
- Norepinephrine

Besides these neurotransmitters, others also send messages in a person's brain. These include GABA, acetylcholine, and glutamate. Scientists are still studying the specifics of what roles each of these chemicals plays in the brain when it comes to depression or other mental health conditions such as anxiety or PTSD (Post-Traumatic Stress Disorder).

Let's learn a little about how our brain cells communicate by using our neurotransmitters. A synapse is a space between two nerve cells. When two cells want to communicate, our neurotransmitters can be packed up and then released from the end of one cell and passed across that space between, destined for the other cell to receive it. As these packaged neurotransmitters travel across that space, postsynaptic cells (the receiving cells) can take up those neurotransmitters in their receptors if they are looking for that specific chemical. For instance, serotonin receptors will aim to pick up serotonin molecules. If there are any excess lingering molecules in that space, the presynaptic cell (the cell sending the neurotransmitters) will gather those molecules and use them in another cell's communication by reprocessing them. Different types of neurotransmitters carry different messages, which play a specific role in creating a person's brain chemistry, including their emotions, memories, thoughts, and mood. An imbalance in the levels of those chemicals is what is theorized to play a huge role in depression and other mental health conditions such as anxiety.

Now this is where psilocybin and magic mushrooms come into the equation. As you learned earlier in this chapter, the chemical psilocin (which psilocybin is converted to when it enters the body) acts on the serotonin receptors in the brain. Therefore, if there is an imbalance in serotonin levels in the person's brain, such as too little serotonin being produced and released by the presynaptic cells, they will feel depressed. When psychedelic mushrooms are consumed, the psilocin that enters the brain will bind to the serotonin receptors, thus leveling serotonin levels in the brain to a normal level. This will then lead a person to feel an increase in their positivity and a decrease in their feelings and symptoms of depression.

Modern Research on Psilocybin Mushrooms

Before we end this chapter, we will spend some time learning about some modern research related to psilocybin. This research has only begun recently, where harsh bans of psilocybin mushrooms have started to be lifted due to the numerous benefits of using them.

1. A study conducted in 2016, published in the Journal of Psychopharmacology (medication and drugs for mental health), gave cancer patients suffering from depression a dose of psilocybin (the active chemical that provides us with the effects of magic mushrooms) for six months. They revisited them six

months later to find that all of them reported lower levels of depression.

2. Another study was done in 2014, which looked at the use of magic mushrooms for addiction treatment. This study focused on those who were addicted to nicotine in the form of smoking cigarettes. Six months of treatment with magic mushrooms later, the study found that eighty percent of these patients had quit smoking for good. Compared to regular pharmaceutical drugs prescribed for people who wish to quit smoking, this was much higher as the results of these drugs only report working in thirty-five percent of smokers.

3. A foundation in the United States conducted a study on psilocybin for the treatment of depression in individuals whose depression had previously been resistant to treatments. The results were staggering. 67 percent of the patients were reportedly depression-free after only one week of treatment, and 42 percent of the patients were in depression remission three months after beginning the study.

4. Research done in London, England, looked at the effects of magic mushrooms on the brain by studying the brains of people under the influence of them using a functional magnetic resonance machine or an fMRI. They had two groups, one that took a placebo and one that took real magic mushrooms. The results of this study showed that the drug led to massive levels of connection among areas of the brain that are generally not connected and do not normally share information. The group that took the placebo showed much less communication among different regions of the brain. Scientists concluded that this is likely why the users of magic mushrooms report feeling like they are in a dream-like state of being.

5. A study that followed the study above further explored the effects of magic mushrooms on the brain by looking at their effects on deeper areas. Results showed that psilocin leads to decreased brain activity in a particular area of the brain called the Thalamus. This area of the brain is responsible for restricting and preventing the transmission of signals between certain areas of the brain. Since magic mushrooms lead to decreased activity in this region of the brain, this study explained how being under the influence of magic mushrooms leads to an increased connection between areas, as the Thalamus is unable to stop or control the transmission of these messages.

6. A study conducted in 2011 found that, while it is very difficult to change a person's personality after they have reached adulthood, magic mushrooms are one of the very few things that make this possible. This study showed that after only ingesting magic mushrooms one single time, the users became more open to trying new things and were more open to new experiences for more than a year! There have been very few studies that have found results as staggering as this one. The reason for this change in personality is the effects that psilocybin has on a person's emotions, which in turn impacts their feelings about the world around them, their place in it, their feelings about others, and their feelings about themselves. Since magic mushrooms lead to such a deeply profound experience for their users, this experience has lasting effects on a person. One thing to note about this study was that all of the participants had positive trips. This change in personality cannot be extended to those who have bad trips, but those who have good trips have proven to lead to lasting changes.

7. One study conducted on mice in 2013 showed that after ingesting psilocybin, they had much less of a fear response to a

noise that had previously caused them a lot of fear associated with an electric shock. By being exposed to this drug, they had less fear as their bodies seemed to forget that this noise was something that they were afraid of, and their brains did not associate fear with this noise anymore. The researchers who conducted this study wish to extend these results one day to test small doses of magic mushrooms given to people to treat post-traumatic stress disorder (PTSD).

8. One very famous study was done in the 1960s, in the time of the hippie and before magic mushrooms were deemed an illegal, schedule 1 substance. This study involved giving magic mushrooms to people who were going to attend a church service. There was also a group of control subjects who were given regular mushrooms as a placebo. The patients given magic mushrooms reported that they had felt a spiritually transcendent experience during the church service, along with feeling united with god and feeling sacred. Many of these people also said that this experience had changed their lives forever. They felt as if they had experienced something bigger than themselves and that it had altered their perspective of life for good.

There is still much work to be done on the political front when it comes to magic mushrooms and psilocybin, as it is still listed as a Schedule 1 controlled substance in the United States and is banned in most of the world. This is still the case despite these and other studies that show the countless benefits they can provide, with minimal side effects. Most of the other drugs in this category have no shown benefits in the medical industry and come with many negative side effects, along with a huge prevalence of being abused and leading to addiction.

Chapter Four: Grow Kits

For many people, the draw of the mushroom kit and the ease with which one can set up the grow box outweigh the cost of such a kit. The hard work of creating substrate, inoculation, and waiting for colonization has been done for you already. A typical grow kit comes with a substrate that has already been colonized to streamline the growing process.

These are ideal for those who are short on time or would prefer to test a specific strain or to have a quick, fun project to focus on with little commitment or effort. Many use the Psilocybe cubensis grow kits when they do not want to go through adding the mushroom spores themselves. Many kits are available in different varieties, each with its different flavor notes and strength. You can grow many flushes of tasty and beautiful mushrooms by adding a little bit of water, air, and light.

Mushroom kits come with several different types of substrates that feed different types of mushrooms. Some mushrooms grow better on wood chips or a wooden log, while others grow better on straw. It is good practice to get familiar with reading reviews on companies and their products should you feel the need to look into using a grow kit. The most common substrate that comes with a grow kit is a block of sterilized sawdust and wood chips. While some suppliers sell bags of pre-pasteurized straw, the risk of contamination is still much higher than if you pasteurize at home. Often, it is better to avoid kits that contain these.

How Do They Work?

Mushroom grow kits are, for the lucky ones, low-maintenance and easy to use. All that is required is to keep it watered, give it access to fresh air, and give it good lighting. To optimize the growth of your mushrooms, expose the kit to cold temperatures for twelve to twenty-four hours before removing it and proceeding with regular care. While this is not a necessity, the cold does simulate the temperatures required to encourage rapid growth before winter.

While the directives which come along with your kit will go into more detail on the care of your mycelium, below is an overview of what you can expect to do once the box arrives at your door.

1. **Wood chip block/sawdust**. Submerge your block in filtered water and place it into the freezer for no longer than twenty-four hours: any longer and the risk of killing your mycelium increases. Take out the block from the refrigerator and place it in a protected, well-lit area. Not direct sunlight. Keep an eye on your block; it should not dry out. (Bonus tip: keep the block in a place that is well-ventilated but not in the direct path of a breeze or turbulent airflow, as this could cause unwanted mold spores and bacteria to contaminate your block.) Your mushrooms should appear within a few days.

2. **Wooden log**. Submerge your log into cold water for no longer than twenty-four hours: any longer, and the risk of killing your mycelium increases. Remove it from the water and place it someplace off the floor in a sheltered spot indoors. (Bonus tip: While you can place the log outside, as often this is the intended use, keeping it indoors is the safer bet, especially as a beginner. Be sure to keep your pets away from your log as their fur is riddled with contaminants.) Keep your log damp, and your mushrooms will sprout within a few days.

Some mushroom kits will produce several flushes of mushrooms, so continue watering your kit as per the accompanying instructions. Many kits will yield mushrooms every couple of weeks for anywhere from two months to a year. After the kit has been exhausted, many prefer to remove it from the packaging and toss it into the garden or compost heap. Sometimes, the mycelium will take in the new environment, and you will see new growth by the following spring.

It is important to note that the quality of the mushroom may not be perfect nor advisable to be consumed unless you are comfortable identifying your mushroom. With the new growth exposed to many contaminants, it could prove unsafe for. Grow kits (also known as mycelium boxes) come ready to use. They contain substrate that has been pre-inoculated, and in many cases, the substrate has already been colonized, and mycelium has formed.

Following is a typical step-by-step guide on how to use these kits:

Your mycelium box should be filled with a pre-inoculated (pre-grown mycelium of the *Psilocybe cubensis* species) and a few extras to make use easier.

The set contains:

1. Colonized substrate in a plastic container
2. A filter bag and two paper clips

Instructions:

1. Soak your substrate! Mushrooms are 90% water. Therefore, they need water to grow. Open a corner of your container, and with a gentle stream, fill it until the substrate is covered. Many sets allow for the use of tap water. My recommendation is to use filtered water. Close the lid and let sit for twelve hours.

2. When the time has elapsed, open a corner of your container and pour out the excess water.

3. Remove (and keep) the lid from your container, placing the container inside the filter bag. Fold the top of the filter bag over and fasten with the two paper clips. Place the bag in a warm spot, out of direct sunlight.

4. To mist, open a small corner of the bag wide enough for the nozzle of your bottle. Reseal your bag, and keep it closed. Mushrooms will appear within a week.

Harvesting Your Grow Kit:

Your mushrooms are ready to be harvested when the veil underneath the head or cap of the mushroom has just started to tear. The cap should not open fully. By then, it is too late. Use clean scissors to cut close to the base of the stem. Many people prefer to pinch the base, twist, and pull. However, this disturbs the substrate and the smaller mushrooms that are still growing. After harvesting, your kit can be used again. Most often, your kit will yield up to four to five flushes of mushrooms before your substrate is depleted. You can let the smaller mushrooms grow to maturity before soaking your substrate again, as in step one (1). Continue as before by putting it in the filter bag. Depending on the environmental conditions and the variety of mushrooms you chose, seeing results can take anywhere from five days to two weeks. Temperatures that fluctuate too much or are too far above or below the ideal range will slow growth or even lead to mycelium death.

Why Utilize Growing Kits?

There are a number of benefits to utilizing mushroom kits.

1. The kit requires nominal energy. There is no pasteurizing or heavy manual labor. No drilling or hammering.

Everything has been done for you. All that is left is water, an ideal location, and some patience.

2. Compared to purchasing your edible mushrooms at a store, the kits are a more cost-effective choice. Similarly, should you decide to grow psilocybin mushrooms from kits short-term, the kit is also a boundless way to do that.

3. These kits are also educational. You can choose from various mushrooms and see how they grow and how each is affected by several different environmental variables.

4. Growing your mushrooms from a dependable kit at your home is safe. The keyword here is "reputable." Ensure that you do your research as far as vendors go. It is much safer to grow your own at home than it would be to risk picking wild mushrooms when you are not 100% sure of species. (The risk here is getting poisoned by what you pick.) Getting an organic kit also reduces the likelihood of exposure to other harmful chemicals or pesticides.

5. Given the limitations of the kit and the harvest's size compared to growing from scratch, the kits are a fun, easy, and often rewarding experience.

Drawbacks of Grow Kits

Certainly, the kits are not without criticism. Listed are some drawbacks to purchasing and using a mushroom grow kit:

1. The initial expense (not unlike growing from scratch) could quickly start racking up if you are not aware of where and what type of kit you purchase. While the kit does provide you with several flushes, there is still the initial chunk of cash laid out. A good quality kit will cost approximately $30 along with shipping. Some will be slightly cheaper, but beware when

deciding on the more expensive ones that go for upwards of $50. You could find many of these more affordable elsewhere. That does not mean that you should skimp on quality, though.

2. While the kits will provide you with a fair volume of mushrooms with several flushes, the kit is not unlimited. Growing from scratch will yield more product in the long run. Kits aren't meant for large-scale production and distribution.

3. You run the risk of buying poor quality. Some kits (especially if the vendor is unrated or poorly rated) run the risk of not growing. It could be contaminated at the outset or not be the type of mushroom advertised on the box.

The biggest drawback (on both growing from scratch and growing from a kit) is the time it takes. Many who purchase kits expect instant results. It will still take a few weeks to grow, regardless. Despite their seeming convenience, grow kits are widely considered to be a waste of money. While they tend to work out the same as purchasing everything you will need to grow from scratch, a kit is highly unreliable, and many users report that the results are mostly inconsistent. The kits are much more prone to contamination and failure as a result. While still fun to experiment with, purchasing a kit will not teach you how to grow from scratch.

Where to Purchase Organic Mushroom Rising Kits

Should you prefer to start with a mushroom grow kit, the better option is to support your local businesses before ordering online. Below are some places you could buy your mushroom kit. These stores would, if psilocybin mushrooms are illegal in your state/country, only supply edible and medicinal mushrooms:

1. Garden and Home stores. These places will also sell the items required to grow your own mushrooms from scratch.

2. Natural/organic food stores, or stores that specialize in (often gourmet) cooking.

3. Animal husbandry stores.

4. Most notably, you can purchase from the local mushroom growers. In places where psilocybin is still illegal, you will only find edible or medicinal mushrooms from these vendors.

For psilocybin varieties, your safest bet is online through a reputable, highly-rated seller. If you do not do your research well enough, chances are you may end up with a strain that you did not want, or an empty syringe.

Chapter Five: How to Grow Psilocybin Mushrooms

By this point in the book, you should have a strong understanding of all things psilocybin mushroom-related, including the science behind it all, the effects it has to offer, and some of its many uses. This chapter will spend quite a bit of time explaining how to grow your psilocybin mushrooms at home. Keep in mind that this is highly illegal in certain countries, so if you live in a country with strict psilocybin mushroom laws, I do not advise you to do this. On the flip side, there are numerous countries where it's legal for psilocybin mushrooms to be grown. Some countries will allow you to own psilocybin mushroom spores but not the actual mushrooms themselves. Before you start growing your own, make sure you do enough research for the country you reside in.

The first topic we will look into in this chapter is where you can buy your own kits to grow psilocybin mushrooms. This is the easiest way for beginners to grow them as it will guarantee you that the mushroom you are going to grow is the type of mushroom you want. Since there are thousands of different types of psilocybin mushrooms, harvesting them in the wild and growing them in your home is dangerous as you may misidentify it for another type of mushroom.

Where to Buy Psilocybin Mushroom Growing Kits

If you have decided that using kits to grow magic mushrooms is the best way, you are likely wondering how you can find these. This will depend on where in the world you are located, as it is much more difficult in some places than in others. There is an extensive list of websites where you can buy magic mushroom spores or magic mushroom growing kits when you perform a Google search. The tricky part will be finding out whether they deliver to your location and how much this will cost. Below is a list of the most popular websites from which to buy magic mushroom spores or growing kits:

- Magic-mushrooms-shop.com

- Micro-supply.com
- Lilshopofspores.com
- Happytripsolutions.net
- Sporeworks.com
- Trufflemagic.com

This list is not exhaustive as there are many more, though these are the most popular. The last one on the list, "trufflemagic.com," delivers to the United States, Canada, the UK, and the entirety of Europe. Just be sure that your package will not be held at the border or inspected, as this could lead to consequences for you, depending on where you live.

Growing Mushrooms from Scratch

As an alternative to buying a kit, some other ways will allow you to grow your own mushrooms from scratch! Growing them from scratch takes more attention and time, but it will definitely be more rewarding, and it will also lead to a healthier crop and allow you to have more control over how your crop turns out.

If you are growing your own mushrooms from scratch, you will need to buy a spore syringe. You can get these from various suppliers, which will contain the cells from which your mushrooms will grow. When buying this, you can choose from various strains, depending on what you are looking for. As we discussed earlier, some good varieties that are best for beginners include Psilocybe Cubensis and Golden Teacher.

To grow them on your own, you will need to have some rice flour, your spore syringe, water that is suitable for drinking, and Vermiculite, a substance commonly used in gardening that is a combination of several minerals which will help your mushrooms to grow. This can be purchased in a garden store near you. Once you have everything you need, growing them is pretty simple. You will combine your ingredients, minus the spores, and this will form your growing medium. Then, you will insert your spores into this medium, which will give them a nice place to grow. You can do this in a glass jar. Once you see them beginning to grow, you will transfer your product to a better-growing chamber, and then you can watch them develop before your eyes.

Searching for Psilocybin Mushrooms on Your Own

The different species of mushrooms cannot be distinguished solely based on appearance since there are so many different colors, shapes, sizes, and overall varieties of magic mushrooms in the wild.

How to Pick Wild Psilocybin Mushrooms

When it comes to picking mushrooms, it may seem self-explanatory, but there is some technique involved so that you do not rip them, crush them, or otherwise damage them in any way. They have been growing for some time, and they need to be treated delicately, as they are quite fragile from a physical standpoint. You also do not want to damage the growing medium so that another batch of mushrooms or fungus of some sort will be able to grow there.

To pick mushrooms, you want to carefully and gently separate them from whatever growing medium they are currently in. When you are going to pick your mushrooms, the technique is called "twist and pull." Grab onto the bottom of the stem gently with your thumb and your first finger. Without squeezing too firmly, twist and pull the stem out of the growing medium. You will feel the stem begin to loosen from the soil or moss (or wherever it is growing). Continue to pull it in this way, but if it proves difficult, avoid squeezing too firmly. Practice this with one mushroom at a time so that the growing medium stays intact. Picking the mushrooms should not damage what is left behind. As you practice this, it will become easier and easier. It may seem time-consuming, but it is worth it for the beautiful mushrooms that will result.

How Exactly are Psilocybin Mushrooms Grown?

Mushrooms have been growing in the wild since the beginning of time, as they do not need any help from us humans to do so. As long as the conditions for their growth are right, they can grow. Mushrooms begin from tiny cells that are invisible to the naked human eye. These cells reproduce when they are provided with enough of their preferred "food" and eventually grow into mushrooms. Mushrooms are a kind of fungus, not a kind of plant, so they grow from cells and not from seeds like plants do. These cells, called Spores, can be found in the forest, soil on farms, and tree bark, among other places. When these spores meet moisture, humidity, darkness, and nutrients such as wood, water, straw, grains, and other things of this variety found in nature, they will begin to reproduce rapidly, and mushrooms will eventually grow in this place. The only difference between magic mushrooms and regular mushrooms is that the magic mushrooms contain the psychedelic chemical compound, and others do not.

How they grow and reproduce are the same, however. Mushrooms reproduce in a fascinating fashion. As I mentioned, they do not spread seeds as plants do. Mushrooms are covered in their spores, which contain their genetic information. By having their spores all over them, they can easily be spread around by the wind, by getting caught on the fur or feathers of animals that brush by them, or by being splashed around in the rain. When this happens, the spores will land in an area that is hopefully conducive to their growth, and then they will be able to get the nutrients they need to grow tall and strong, allowing the parent mushroom to pass on its genes. The interesting thing about mushrooms, though, is that they have found a way to get past the problem of a wind-free day or week. Some mushrooms can create their own wind, which they use to spread their spores all over the forest floor. They create wind by increasing the amount of water on their surface, leading to an increase in evaporation, creating vapor above them. This water vapor contains the spores that were covering the mushroom cap. Once in the water vapor created by evaporation, the cool air above the mushrooms lifts and spreads the spores, sending them off to spread over the forest floor in hopes of finding a great place to land and grow.

Some people have been turned off by the prospect of going out and looking for mushrooms, though this was how ingesting magic mushrooms began since they are present in the wild without any intervention from humans. This presents several risks, such as ingesting a poisonous mushroom erroneously or having to dig through cow dung in hopes of finding some, not to mention consuming some of the cow dung that the mushrooms were found growing in. If you wish to grow magic mushrooms on your own due to any of these reasons or any other reasons that I have not mentioned, it is quite possible to grow your own instead of foraging for them.

Cultivation Methods

There are numerous different types of magic mushroom cultivation methods. Here, we will cover three popular methods for more experienced growers. Then, in the step-by-step instructions, we will be learning about a more beginner-level cultivation method. Regardless of the difficulty, it is still great to know different ways to do this once you have some experience under your belt.

Rye Grain Tek

This cultivation method uses rye grain due to its ability to hold more water, which will give more significant flushes. Previous to utilizing the rye, soak it in a jar for one day (minimum 24 hours) filled with water. Pour the water out (the water will be yellow at this point) and then use a small amount of water to boil the rye. Drain, then fill it back into the jars. Be sure not to fill the jar completely; leave enough space so you can still shake the contents of the jar. Then, insert 2 – 3cc of spores into it using a syringe. Use sterile material to cover the hole in the lid and shake the jars as much as you can so the spread of the spores is even throughout the rye. After this, all you have to do is wait, as colonization will take anywhere between 9 to 21 days.

Popcorn Tek

The popcorn tek method is not the most popular compared to other methods, as some experts believe that it doesn't colonize as nicely as rye does. However, there are many people that swear by this method. Hint here, don't use popcorn; simple corn will be enough! Take your corn and soak it in water for one day (at least 24 hours), drain it, and place the corn in a pressure cooker for about 45 to 60 minutes. If you don't have a pressure cooker, you can replace this step by simmering the corn in a pan and stirring it often to avoid burning on the bottom. Then, drain out the water and roll your corn in a dry cloth or towel. Dry out the corn as much as you can. Then, put your corn into jars and make sure it has a filter in there as you will have to cook them again, and the gas has to have some way of getting out.

Bulk Growing

You will require anywhere between 3 to 6 colonized jars and a large tub of fresh manure for this cultivation method. The ratio of manure to spawn needs to be 3:1 or 2:1 if you'd like it to be less smelly. An alternative to manure that you can use is coir. The tub you use must have holes in the bottom and the side of the tub. Take your manure and place it into your tub until it fills past the bottom set of holes. Take your jars and shake them to break up the spawn evenly. Prepare 1 to 2 jars to put aside for later on, and mix the rest of your jars into the substrate evenly. Ensure your substrate is even, and then place the content from your jars to form a top layer. You can now put the lid back on your tub and leave it in a dark room. You can wrap a towel around the tub to make sure no light gets in. Now, you will have to wait for five days. DO NOT move or open it during this time. If you do, you may cause contamination or failure. Wait until 5 days have passed, then check if your substrate has fully colonized. If it hasn't, wait three more days and see.

Tools You Will Need

If you are growing your mushrooms indoors, you will first need to determine which species and strain you will want to grow. The websites provided earlier should have a large selection for you, but the most popular strain is Psilocybe Cubensis B+, which we learned about earlier in this book. Again, there are thousands of different psilocybin mushroom strains, so do your research and decide which type is the most suitable for you. Here are the tools and ingredients you will need:

Ingredients:

- Drinking water
- Vermiculite (medium or fine)
- Organic brown rice flour
- Spore syringe (10 to 12 cc)

Equipment:

- Mist spray bottle
- Perlite
- Drill with ¼ inch drill bit
- Clear plastic storage box (anywhere from 50L to 115L)
- Micropore tape
- Small towel (or paper towels)
- Cooking pot with a tight lid (large) for steaming
- Tinfoil, heavy-duty
- Strainer
- Mixing bowl
- Measuring cups
- Hammer and small nail
- 12 half-pint jars with lids (mason jars or canning jars)

Hygiene Supplies:

- Still air or glove box
- Surgical mask

- Sterilized latex gloves
- Air sanitizer
- Surface disinfectant
- Butane/propane torch lighter
- Rubbing alcohol

Growing Your Own Psilocybin Mushrooms in 6 Steps

Growing mushrooms at home is a pleasant and perhaps even profitable hobby. Creating an environment that provides the fungus with optimal underlying conditions and supplements can provide an abundant yield of mushrooms. You can also grow a variety of family mushrooms and shiitake at home, not just psychedelic varieties. However, mushrooms have different growing needs.

Light:

Fungi can't extract nutrients from the sun as green plants do, so they don't need light. However, mushrooms don't necessarily need a dark environment to grow. The preferred place for mushroom growth is in the dark simply because darkness retains the moisture needed to reproduce the fungal spores.

Humidity:

Fungi, like all mushrooms, bloom in a humid environment. Ordinary mushrooms need to be in an environment with 80 – 90% humidity.

Temperature:

Mushrooms can grow at temperatures between 40 and 90 F. Radiators or fans may be needed to create a controlled state where fungi must grow indoors.

Step 1: Preparation

1. Prepare Jars:

Make four holes in each of the lids with the hammer and nail (which should be cleaned with alcohol to disinfect).

2. Preparation of the substratum:

Add 2/3 cup vermiculite and 1/4 cup of water (per jar you will use) in the mixing bowl. Use the disinfected strainer to remove excess water.

Apply 1/4 cup of brown rice flour (per jar you will use) to the bowl and stir with moist vermiculite.

3. Fill Jars:

Be careful not to stack too closely; fill the jars within half an inch of the rims.

Sterilize the top half inch with rubbing alcohol.

Top off your jars with a dry vermiculite layer for contaminant protection of the substratum.

4. Sterilize with steam:

Screw the lids on securely and cover the jars with tin foil. Ensure that the foil is wrapped tightly and securely around the surface of the vessels so that the holes do not get filled water and condensation.

Put a small tray into the base of the big pot and place the jars on top, so that they do not touch the floor.

Add tap water to the pot until it reaches about halfway up the jars, and then bring the water to a boil, making sure the jars are upright.

Once boiling, reduce to a simmer and place the lid tightly on the pot for 75-90 minutes and leave to steam. If the pot becomes dry, fill it with hot tap water.

Note: Some farmers prefer to use a pressure cooker instead of a pot to sterilize their jars.

5. Allow it to cool:

Leave the foil-covered jars in the pot overnight after steaming, so that they cool down fully. Before beginning the next step, the jars must be at room temperature.

Step 2: Inoculation

1. Prepare and sanitize syringe:

Use a lighter to heat the needle length until it is red and hot. Allow it to cool down and dry with alcohol so that your hands do not touch it.

Squeeze the plunger and shake the syringe to disperse the magic mushroom spores uniformly.

Note: Take great care to prevent contamination of your syringe. The surest way is by placing the syringe in a disinfected quiet air or glove box, and also using sterilized latex gloves and a surgical mask.

2. Inject spores:

Remove the foil off the first of your jars and insert the syringe in one of the holes.

Inject around 1/4 cc of the spore solution into the first hole.

Repeat with the other 3 holes, making sure to clean the needle with alcohol between each one.

Repeat the process of inoculation for the remainder of the jars, sterilizing the needle with alcohol after each one.

Step 3: Colonization

1. Wait for the mycelium:

Remove all tin foil and place your inoculated jars somewhere. Be sure that they are kept out of direct sunlight. Also, make sure that they are kept in an environment where the temperature is 70-80 ° F (room temperature).

White, fluffy-looking mycelium should start to spread from inoculation areas after between seven and 14 days.

Note: Watch for signs of infection, including strange colors and smells, and immediately remove suspicious bottles. If you are uncertain if a container is infected, always be careful even if the substrate is otherwise healthy as some pollutants can kill humans.

2. Consolidate:

You should have successfully colonized the jars after three to four weeks if all goes well.

Step 4: Setting Up the Grow Chamber

1. Make a shotgun fruiting chamber:

Take your plastic storage container and drill 1/2-inch holes, about two inches apart, on all four sides, on the base, and on the wall. This is where the fruiting chamber gets its name, as the holes resemble the spray that a shotgun produces.

Set the box on four stable objects arranged underneath at the corners to allow air to flow. You will also want to cover the surface underneath the box to protect against leakage of moisture.

Note: The shotgun fruiting chamber is far from the best design, but it is easy, fast, and good for beginners. You might want to seek alternatives later.

2. Perlite added:

Place your perlite in a strainer and run it to soak under the cold tap.

Allow it to drain until no drips remain and scatter over the base of your chamber.

Repeat for a perlite layer approximately 4-5 inches deep.

Step 5: Fruiting

1. "Birth" of colonized mediums (or "cakes"):

While wearing sterilized gloves, open your jars and remove each layer of dry vermiculite, so as to avoid damaging your substrates, or "cakes."

Invert every jar and tap the disinfected surface to release the cakes.

2. Ensure to Dunk the Cakes:

Rinse the cakes under a chilly tap one at a time to remove loose vermiculite.

Fill a pot with cool water and put the cakes inside. They will float, so place something (such as another, smaller pot) on top so that they are submerged just under the water.

Allow the cakes to rehydrate at room temperature for up to 24 hours.

3. Roll the Cakes:

Remove cakes and put them on a disinfected surface.

Fill your mixing bowl with dry vermiculite.

One by one, coat the cakes in vermiculite.

4. Move to the grow chamber:

For each of your cakes, cut a square of tin foil, large enough for them to rest on without touching the perlite.

Spread these uniformly in the growing chamber.

Place the cakes on top and gently mist the chamber with your spray bottle.

Fan the chamber with the lid a few times, before placing the lid on top.

5. Optimizing and tracking conditions:

Mist the chamber about four times per day so as to keep moisture levels up but be careful not to water your cakes.

To increase airflow, fan with the lid up to six times a day, particularly after misting.

Note: Indirect or ambient lighting is perfect during the day. Mycelium requires just a little light to see where the open air is and where mushrooms are to be made.

Step 6: Harvesting

1. Watch out for the Fruits:

The mushroom or fruit appears as tiny white bumps until they sprout into "sticks." They're ready to harvest after 5-12 days.

2. Choose your fruit:

Slice the mushrooms close to the cake to remove when ready. Don't wait until they finish their development, as they start to lose power as they mature.

Note: Mushrooms are best picked just before the veil falls. They will have small, conical caps and covered gills at this stage.

Storage

Psilocybin mushrooms tend to go bad in the refrigerator within a couple of weeks. So, if you're going to use them for micro-dosing or just want to save them for later, consider storage. Drying is the most efficient form of long-term storage. This should keep them strong for two to three years, while keeping them cool, dark, and dry. If stored in the freezer, they will last for quite a while also. One of the best ways to dry your mushrooms is by leaving them outside on a sheet of paper for days, perhaps in front of a fan. The most successful approach is by far the use of a dehydrator, but it can be expensive.

Chapter Six: Health Benefits of Psilocybin Mushrooms

Psilocybin mushrooms may be the next big thing for holistic treatment and well-being. There are over 200 psychoactive properties of these mushrooms, and they have been used ceremonially for several centuries in different parts of the world. Still, only a few decades ago, the western world discovered their remarkable healing effects, both medicinal, psychological, and emotional. Numerous studies have shown that hallucinogenic mushrooms are far from what governments consider them to be. From the outset, mushrooms containing psilocybin have been used for psychotherapeutic reasons. However, due to the increasing popularity of leisure activities and misunderstood effects, medical use was banned. In the 1970s after 30 years of suspension, the use of psilocybin was again authorized for research purposes.

In contrast, in other countries, such as most of Europe and Australia, psilocybin mushrooms are entirely illegal. Therefore, it is essential to confirm the laws of hallucinogenic mushrooms in different countries. The psilocybin mushroom can be eaten raw or brewed in drinks. After ingestion, psilocybin is rapidly metabolized in the liver and activated by psilocin, circulating in the bloodstream and the brain. When it reaches the brain, it is associated with the petrochemical receptors of serotonin. These receptors are located in the mind and are hosted by neurons, which, if excited, cause an increase in the brain's activity involved in memory, mood, behavior, and emotions.

As Medication at a Microdose

The active hallucinogenic component of magic mushrooms is psilocybin, producing a noticeable effect when consumed in quantities between 0.2 and 0.5 g. However, this differs between individuals. A moderate portion of 1-2.5 g, taken orally, usually causes a trip that lasts from 3 to 6 hours. Psilocybin is processed into psilocin, and both appear to be equally dynamic in the transmission of hallucinogenic experiences. The psilocybin and its psilocin metabolite act mainly with serotonin receptors in the brain.

What to Expect

A typical trip on mushrooms (1-2.5 g) involves a range of experiences and a change in psychological behavior in the structure of "hypnagogic experiences." This is commonly described as brain awakening, and in many ways is similar to sleep. Perceptual changes, for example, fantasies, synesthesia (for example, tasting sounds), dynamic changes, and a distorted sense of time, are generally normal for a mushroom journey. There may be changes in visual recognition, such as radiation around lights, geometric objects, and illustrations when the eyes are closed. Your contemplations and feelings will also begin to change. You are expected to be sensitive to the thoughts and feelings that you will generally avoid in your daily existence.

Very often, there is a sense of amazement about one's environment, a deeper interest in other people, as well as a sense of harmony and communion with the world. Robust, magnificent, and terrifying feelings can arise. It is advisable not to avoid these emotions, but to let them take their course. Physical symptoms may vary in individuals and include changes to the pulse, changes in blood pressure, dilated tendon reflexes, tremors, dilated pupils, and anxiety or excitement.

Stimulates the Growth of New Brain Cells

Research from the University of South Florida published in 2013 investigated the effects of psilocybin mushrooms on mice with fear. What they found surprised them. The leader of the study, Dr. Briony Catlow, of the Lieber Institute for Brain Development, said, "memory, learning, and the ability to learn that a stimulus that has previously been dangerous is no longer a danger; it all depends on the brain's ability to change its connections. We believe that neuroplasticity plays a crucial role in psilocybin's tendency to accelerate the extinction of fear. It is highly possible that in the future we will continue these studies since many interesting questions have come up from these experiments. There is hope that we can extend the findings to humans in clinical trials."

Psilocybin Helps Treat Mood Disorders

Psilocybin can significantly reduce the symptoms of mental health problems, both in men and women. Recently, researchers on this topic have evaluated the therapeutic potential of psilocybin on reducing disturbances to a person's state of mind. In one study, psilocybin significantly improved mood and reduced anxiety in patients with incurable cancer. Healthy volunteers also improved their mood by decreasing the responsiveness of the amygdala, an area of the brain that is primarily concerned with creating a positive attitude.

Relieves the Symptoms of Obsessive-Compulsive Disorder

Obsessive-compulsive disorder is a mental disorder that often occurs in patients who also suffer with schizophrenia, bipolar disorder, and other forms of mental illness. A study conducted by the Ari University in 2006 found that psilocybin mushrooms are very effective in alleviating the symptoms of this disorder.

Psilocybin Can Aid in the Treatment of Substance Abuse

Psilocybin mushrooms are the latest therapeutic alternative for the treatment of disorders associated with substance abuse and addiction to alcohol and drugs. Very recent research on smoking shows that psilocybin is effective in the fight against smoking. For those who smoke, this substance can have a surprising effect on quitting without causing side effects. Psilocybin, as part of an extended treatment plan, showed promising results in the treatment of alcoholism with non-clinical methods in a recent 2015 review that reported a significant reduction in alcohol consumption when psilocybin was used as a planned part of treatment.

In another recent study, 2 or 3 treatment sessions of Psilo-Cybina as part of a larger cognitive-behavioral treatment plan has had an 80% success rate in the treatment of nicotine withdrawal.

It Relieves Anxiety

In research conducted in 2011, scientists discovered that in advanced-stage patients, psilocybin mushrooms calm anxiety drastically after administration.

Connect the Brain in New Ways.

Although psilocybin mushrooms are generally considered dangerous drugs with no medical value in society, an increasing number of studies have led to a different view. In 2015, neurologist Nick Jikomes stated that psilocybin mushrooms help cure habitual drug addiction such as with nicotine and cocaine. Functional magnetic resonance imaging was performed during a psychedelic experience caused by psilocybin fungi. It is believed that these "psilocybin mushrooms" connect the various receptors, providing a smooth ion surface between the different parts of the brain. Research on this is just beginning to explain the remarkable ability psilocybin mushrooms have to cure addiction. We will undoubtedly see more and more medical applications for this ancient medicine in the future.

Treating Depression

Studies have shown that psilocybin fungi are effective in treating absolute blood pressure and treating post-traumatic stress disorder. A prestigious research team in London recently conducted a study suggesting that psilocybin could be used to treat major depression.

Only an hour after the second dose, depression was reduced significantly in almost all patients, with 8 of 12 patients showing no signs of depression. After three months, it was recorded that five patients were still free from depression, and the remaining four had a "mild to moderate" depression rate.

Psilocybin in the Treatment of Cluster Headaches and Migraine

Cluster migraines are often referred to as the most problematic and irritating type of brain pain. They are more extreme than migraines but usually don't last long. Night headaches, in most cases, are more intense than cluster pain attacks during the day, but both disturb the life of the individual in general. To date, no systematic studies have been published describing the potential treatment of psilocybin for headaches. However, numerous anecdotal reports have drawn the attention of the therapeutic network. In the mid-2000s, medical experts began to pay attention to psilocybin and LSD as possible treatments for cluster brain disorder after a percentage of patients reported a reduction in their symptoms after using psilocybin mushrooms recreationally. An ongoing study has shown that psilocybin can be a more effective treatment for cluster headaches than currently available drugs, and almost half of patients describe this substance as a completely effective treatment.

Final Words

Psilocybin-containing Mushrooms are usually tan, brown, and small. They are often regarded by some people in the wild as botch mushrooms because they are easy to confuse with other mushrooms that are poisonous. Remember, be extremely careful if you're picking mushrooms yourself. It's much safer to grow them yourself after purchasing spores from a reliable vendor. Once again, this is illegal in many places around the world, so do your research on your local area to ensure you're not breaking any laws.

People ordinarily consume psilocybin as a fermented tea or prepare it with nourishment to veil its unpleasant taste in the mouth. Dried mushrooms are crushed by manufacturers into powders and prepared in capsule forms, while some people consume mushrooms with chocolate.

Whichever way you choose to consume your psychedelic mushrooms, please make sure that you do so safely! It's always recommended to have a spotter (a sober friend) nearby to watch you and ensure your safety. It's also very important to consider the set and setting whenever you're planning to consume psychedelics.

As you can see, the research on these fascinating life forms is only just beginning. Undoubtedly, over the next few years more and more studies will be conducted to prove just how powerful and healing these mushrooms can be when taken correctly.

I hope you've enjoyed learning all about psilocybin mushrooms, their effects, and how they can be grown. I wish you the best of luck on the psychedelic and spiritual journey that these mushrooms take you on!

www.ingramcontent.com/pod-product-compliance
Lightning Source LLC
LaVergne TN
LVHW021738060526
838200LV00052B/3347